The Bridge Unburned

J. Aaron Smith

BookLeaf Publishing

India | USA | UK

Presentation by *BookLeaf Publishing*

Web: www.bookleafpub.com

E-mail: info@bookleafpub.com

ISBN: 9789363305755

First edition 2024

For Emily "Indy" Martin

Without you, I would not have found me.

ACKNOWLEDGEMENT

Thank you to everyone at Poetic Underground KC for embracing my words. The countless workshops and hours you donate of yourselves to encourage both written and spoken expression. Mostly for providing a safe space and a brave space.

I Love You.

You may never swim in the sound of my voice
You might only devour my words with your eyes
I may never feel the colors of your soul
I may never stain you with mine
Tell me about your dreams, and favorite songs
Tell me about your fears, and favorite books
Let everyone else celebrate your virtues
Know that I will celebrate your flaws
Because you are the only *you* there has ever
been

And I love you

You are Beautiful

You are beautiful

You are beautiful when your voice cracks
When butterflies try to climb out of your chest
and swarm into the waiting arms of the person
before you
You are beautiful when you sigh
when your heart is exhausted from the knives
left in your breast
Agitating the bruises that left your body years
ago
and still stain your jaded heart
You are beautiful when you laugh
When fairies are born from your mirth
And they dance inside everything your voice
touches
You are beautiful when you speak
When your truth is born from your lips
To climb into my soul and unlock the shackles
of my prison
You are beautiful when you imagine
When your perfect mind doesn't notice
That I am referring to you everytime I say:

You are beautiful.

Your Words

Did you trade a silver spoon for a switchblade

Because your tongue pierces the shell I hide
within

Cuts down my mountains like tissue paper

And lets your light
A thousand stars pressing against my emptiness

The darkness within bleeds out

Ink spilling onto pages stained with oceans of
"wish you were still here"

I let the tides pull the magic from your lips

And I hang from the moon

Waiting to taste

Your words

You are Everything

Let me fall in love with nothing
Let me fall in love with your missing laugh
Because I need to love life
More than life hated you
I understood you
You accepted me
So let me fall in love with the absence of you
Let me fall in love with a life
That no longer includes the shape of you
You were everything
You are everything
Since I collided with your perfect soul
My heart has always whispered:

Nothing can replace you.

So…

Let me fall in love with nothing.

Breathe into Me

You took away my breath with your lips
Not from touching my skin with yours
But by forming the words that taste like truth
And lies
And the gray things in between

You exhaled the moments that shook the
universe
The earthquakes that leveled your soul
And left you broken in a pool of your own
perfection
The tremors of love that made me understand
The reason mortals dance naked in moonbeams
I find myself stained by the colors of your soul
The bright vivid india inks of your emotions
Shaded with the charcoals of your experience
Forming a picture of the moments
That created this work of life called you
I care not what shape your form takes
For you possess beauty that cannot be seen or
touched
I ache to swim forever in your voice
Your words are Michaelangelo to my marble
heart
And you carve yourself onto me

Shaping me into someone new with each word
And newly born
I do not yet know
How to breathe
Because you took my breath away with your lips

I was Silent

I am sorry
I didn't find you first
Before life pulled us apart
I was loving the wrong person
Except that isn't correct
to love the wrong person is impossible
Everyone deserves Love
I gave my time to the wrong person
I gave my loyalty to the wrong person
I gave my loneliness to the wrong person
And that was my mistake
Giving them so much loneliness
I do love them
But I was comfort to their loneliness
I was not their love
Not their person
So while I was busy trying to love
You were trying too and I wasn't there
You were wounded by love's imposter,
Love does not insult, threaten, maim, injure….

That wasn't love

And I am sorry
I was silent

I am sorry I didn't speak up
Years before this moment
Now I have so many scars

And you have a headstone

A Moment

How long did I know you?
Longer than an eternity
Shorter than a moment
I was infected with you
You were my Anam Cara
True friend, Truest love
But you were sick
And your loop was stronger than my voice
They didn't have a magic pill
to stave your love of the darkness
There was no chemotherapy
for your depression
Doctors could not amputate
your aching heart
Oh, how I wish you told me about all of your
demons
Not just the ones you felt I could face
Now your form is buried deeper than my voice
can reach
You slipped forever into the cold darkness

When you danced one last time with death
And I did not see the chance to cut in
Why do I still love you when you are forever
hers?
Tell me, does she treat you well?
Does she hold you soft in her embrace?
Does her voice calm your frustration?
Does her smile soothe your pain?
Does she accept you for who you are?
Does she love you better…
Than I could?
And will she do the same for me
When I am asked to the final dance?
I will not hate Death
For she is part of life
The very bitter and painful last part
But I will fight her for every breath
I will fight her for every sunrise
I will fight her for every perfect leaf
I will fight her for every heartbeat
My own
And the rhythm of heartbeats
within every imperfect soul I meet
Because once I was one
Now I am two
For you exist within me
I can't stop our one-ended conversation
And you can't answer
You are dancing in the dark

Twisted up in the Moon
Scattered like stars
And I am just eyes on the sunset
Watching the world orbit the Sun
Swimming in this absence of you
This life
Longer than an eternity
Shorter than a moment

Rose Leaves

I want to dive in with both hands standing
And watch it slip and splash
Like stained glass over eons
To bite and taste the flesh of innocence
Forgive, but not to pierce the skin
But to ignite souls gem with a bit of hot light
Tinting its color a bit more real and deep
To breathe in life, before wonder was stifled
To tap the sinful aftertaste
Same opium in the dark
I want to fall
A shooting star of sapphire,
To burst into a thousand dust particles
To be carried away by swallows and scissortails
To a dry ivy stained bird bath
Filled with a thousand perfect rose leaves
To remain undisturbed until it ends and after

Porcelain

Maybe if I had teeth
that cut like your words
I could bite my tongue
And let the purest reddest truth out
Can I stain you red
Make you blush
Ace of hearts
King of spades
No suicide today
Deal me the perfect card
For I am playing doubles or nothings
Roll the dice
Snake eyes
And I'm bitten, addicted
I drink to the pain
As I lay and convulse on this mosaic tile
This perfect porcelain pain
A pain I could not paint without you

Taste

Pressure mixture
Lips and skin
Breathe into wanting souls
As I sin for angels
and weep for jealous gods
immune to belief
for belief holds hope
And hope is an ocean of love
An ocean I will never understand
Even as I swim in it
And get lost in the waves

She/Her

Hour is early
Order paid with time
Minutes of caffeine
Seconds unwilling as a red right-hand
rhythmic tics on the cosmic coffee watches
and down the drain it slumbers
Slowly murmuring its waste
Bitter thick and grainy
The city's acrid aftertaste
It whirrs around the darkened eyes
Confused and frightened fools
Who fear the stranger's wrath
When she surely lurks within

The Strawberry Moon

She hangs in the air pale and perfect
The fullness of her naked form pulling me with
her siren song

And I, the ocean, ever reaching upward in hopes
of caressing her form
For as she tiptoes through the stars
My love for her erases the laws of the universe
and the Earth almost releases me
On the first lazy night of Summer
The moon, full and lonely, lowered herself from
her lofty perch and beckoned
I, the ocean, found the courage to leap up a
cascade of infinite salty drops
leaving the fish and whales floundering and
confused in my dry seabed
I, the ocean, shed tears of joy as I enveloped her
perfect heavenly body
The coldness of space would freeze my lazy
waves around her
But I did not care
As I became permanently entangled with her
gravity and embraced every inch of her valleys
and mountains

And though she is now shaded blue with the
color of my heart
You can still see the blush of her cheeks from
when I wrapped myself around her
Together we would carve the sky as she moved
across the heavens

And I, the whimpering wolf, would howl at the
distance the moon is from my lips
Knowing a meager beast is no match for the
ocean's embrace
I, the whimpering wolf, would cry each night as
she danced across the darkness
Forever out of reach
She would still comfort me once a month with
her cheshire grin
Reminding me even a small beast silhouetted by
her perfection is beauty in her shadow
And I would howl

And I, the lover, would paint the whimpering
wolf silhouetted by the moon as a gift for my
now-lost lover
Unable to deliver the token because of the
ocean's departure and the great impassable
chasm left behind
The lover's lover lies alone naked and perfect on
a distant shore gazing at the strawberry moon
suspended in the sky

Jealous and lonely as the wolf
I, the lover, would reminisce about the nights we
traced moonbeams under satin sheets, fingers
chasing heaven and howling our own soft cry to
the moon

And I, the poet, would write about the missing
ocean, the whimpering wolf, and the lonely
lovers
I, the poet, would write about all the ways I love
the moon and all the ways I wish she could love
me back

More than Air

I love you more than air
I have heard this phrase before
Or read it in a poem
Or saw it in a play
It seemed so silly then

Before I met you

Before I met you
I needed air to live
And I guess I still do…
I love you more than air
Because while air
Fills my lungs
Gives me life
Powers my voice
Air does not take my breath away when she
laughs
Air does not get so overjoyed she curls up in
excitement
Air does not have your eyes
Eyes that light up a room like the midday sun
Air does not look at me and see all the things I
cannot say

Air did not make me see the universe for the
wonder that it is
So now that I have met you

I understand

I love you more than air

Thank You

Thank you,
For writing all the words I cannot write
Because I have not been you
Thank you for singing
Because the melody is twisted up in my idleness
Thank you for speaking the hard uncomfortable
truths
Because they echo in the locks that bind the
chains around my heart
Thank you for the words you spoke
The words I forgot the shape and order of
Because I was too busy tasting your pain and
love
You have unstoppered the words bottled in my
inhibition
And you have freed me from the reluctance I
wasn't aware I had

How do you Know

How do you know they love you?
Is it their smile when they see you walk into a
room?
Is it the way the end of your name always tastes
like an upper inflection?
Is it their eyes the way they smile at your
imperfect form?
Is it the little things they do…
the quirky uniqueness only they possess?
How do you know if you love them?
Do all the little things become vines plunging
into your arteries and tracing your veins back to
the center of your beating heart
Tangling themselves irrevocably in your Soul
Do you feel lighter when they walk into a room?
Do you forget you are supposed to be sad?
Enjoy all those feelings and just trust them
Because while we live, there is always this
intangible unknowing of another heart
That is part of the excitement of love

If you have to know…
You will know when their favorite song plays
And you can't decide whether to skip it or play it
again

You will know by the clothes hidden in forgotten
corners, still stained with their scent
Buckling your knees before work
You will know when they are the night sky
A vast emptiness dotted with pinpoints of light
You will know by the colors missing from the
sunset

I pray you never know
You will only know ...

When they are forever gone.

Before we Kiss

There is something I have to tell you before we
kiss
Before you tangle me up in your beating heart
I will stain our mornings with tears as the sun
splashes light across the world
I will bleed all over you with stories of the
person before you
And I am Sorry
I do want to taste your love
But I am now stained so crimson with missing
her that you will have to know her too
because she twisted her way honeysuckle and
wisteria into my soul

We were four cylinders of chasing the sun
to hide in the midday shadow of the moon
to the sound of the total eclipse of the heart

And she was the music

We were lazy afternoons on back porches
Waiting for sunsets
Devouring books like starving dragons.

And she was the pages

We were rainstorms lying on her bed
Watching movies
Just close enough that you could feel the charge
in the air

And she was lightning

I am sorry that I have to ask for you to
understand her
When she is a headstone
and a grave
And oh so many memories
But her life and laughter set fire to my dark
forest
A forest that now burns as a phoenix of seeds
she planted with her acceptance,
And it grows wild
The flames blazing out of control
Forging the white-hot center of my soul
Creating the light spilling out of my lips
Warning you not to run your ship aground
Upon my melancholy shore

It is the fire of her love that echoes in your
wanting heart
There is no line where I begin and she ends
I will love you
But before we Kiss
I need you to understand
If you want to love me
You will have to love her too

Donum Res Publica

I brought you a gift, I didn't wrap it because you
can not hold it in your hands, but you will be
able to feel it. I will be accused of poor
gift-giving etiquette since the gift I am giving
you has always been yours, but maybe you didn't
know that she was. Perhaps to you she might be
he or them or we,
I am giving you America,
because maybe, like me, you think America
belongs to just a select few people.
She does not. She belongs to the huddled masses
and the wretched.
I am giving you America because I did not
nurture her when I should have.
I did not pay attention to how sick she had
become. Malnourished, depressed, suicidal.
I did not notice her pain each time a freedom
was taken.
Her heart is freedom and she has slowly been
losing slivers of her soul.
I have heard her mumbling to herself, she didn't
feel that she deserved a birthday party this year.
She has been having intrusive thoughts that war
against her beliefs. She has been violent lately.

I am giving you America because you can speak to her and tell her she is beautiful.
Your words can heal her wounds, comfort the bruises left by the Men who abused her.
We don't need to make America great again. She has always been great, because she is not a nation. She is you. She is me.
United we are great, divided we are not.
I need you to raise a lamp to the words at her feet.
Because I am tired and I yearn to breathe free.
The media and propaganda would tell you that you are the blood of America, and she does bleed.
but you are her nerves.
So when she stumbles and falls down, let her know where it hurts. Speak out when she is injured by violence. Temper your outrage with love and compassion. America needs your love, our love.
I do not want to stand in front of a headstone that is etched with the words. Here lies America the beautiful.
I am tired of reading epitaphs.
If we are going to pursue happiness you will have to use your words. Use your voice. Your voice has weight.

I am giving you America because the embers
sparking in your eyes have not burned out. I can
see the fires within you, and I need your fire.
I need your fire, if we are going to burn the
sanctuaries of racism to cinders.
I need the lightning in your voice.
There is a storm brewing and I need your
thunder to shatter the discrimination of the
tempest-tossed who have chosen love without
regard of love's gender or identity.
I need you to be a lighthouse steady and bright
on these rocky shores,
A beacon of light for those who fear the storm to
guide them to calm and safe harbors.
I am giving you America because I was Silent,
But I am speaking now, and I am asking you to
speak.
I am giving you America because I love her, and
I need you to save her from herself.

Anyway

I love you, and before you ignore it,
I know, you don't feel the same,
It won't stop my heart from beating to the
rhythm of your name,
It won't make me less excited to see you,
Just disappointed that this perfection of you
dancing like stars in my eyes,
Is meant to light someone else's fire,
I am happily scorched,
I would be more content if you had already met
your match,
I would be happy if your person swept you up in
a hurricane of kisses,
If you knew love, the kind that twists your soul
wringing out all the awful past like a dishrag that
has been used too long.
You know… the way you twisted out all my
sadness when we kissed,
I don't think you understand how much sadness
you squeezed out of me,
I just hope none of my sadness seeped into you,
And maybe you were in love with the sadness,
That would give me a reason that doesn't make
me wonder if I'm broken,

I am not Sad, I am just taking care of a really big
Sad right now.
I know you don't love me with the same
intensity that I love you.
I can't help it, you are wonderfully intoxicating,
and I am an addict,
I won't ask that you love me back,
That cage is no good for anyone,
But when your soul sighs, always remember,
That, as you are, is the way I love you,
Even when…
especially when, you don't think you deserve it,
I love you anyway.

She is a Leo

She is a Leo
The Moon's cool light splinters across her form
The night stars speak to the shape of her prowess
as each of her muscles dance with grace
She moves sleek and powerful
Weaving in and out of memory
she has claws made of truth
And teeth made of words
She does not chase
She simply is
And she will lay down by the bank
And drink with you if she desires

She is a Leo
Her passionate roar echoes for miles
An announcement that she is here
And she owns all of the atoms her voice touches
Hidden in the echo, a subtle warning
Of claws and teeth and her hunger
A sort of melody that beckons you to walk away
from the herd
Whispering "stand among the tall grass naked
and vulnerable."

She is a Leo

She knows what she desires
She knows that which she hunts
Her teeth find your exposed neck
Her claws dig into your back
In that sweet pain there is a promise that she will
devour you

She is a Leo
And the lion does not sleep tonight

The Trap

I was wandering in the wilds
When I heard a soft cry
I approach the sound as lightly as my hungry
footsteps will allow
There, in a clearing
The source of my new curiosity
A strange contraption filled with so much white
fur and blood-stained steel
When did the dirt grow a mouth?
A small white fox whimpers as I approach
Caught inside so many metal teeth
She struggles as each point of pain grips her
chest
I notice the terror dancing in her eyes
Because I am a Wolf
Scar tattered and hungry
And she is unable to escape and run
I smell the small part of her that wants the pain
to end
But the rest of her
Longs to run free in the wilds from which I
came
Pinned by the clamping steel
She is so vulnerable and soft
It would be so simple

To just sink my teeth in and devour her
I look deep into her pain
Those eyes begging me to set her free…
Or devour…
I ponder as I know she would take either
freedom
And I am starving
So simple
To just give in to my instincts
And what gift have I
For releasing her from her prison?
Just more scars
And more pain
And more hunger
After all
I am a wolf
and there are other foxes
But she looks so deliciously different
She smells different
She feels different
But just a quick bite…
It would be painless for her…
Or at least it would be quick
I edge closer
And I breathe in the fear and the longing
Both scents mingling
Both scents tempting me to fill my mouth with
her flesh
and consume her last moans

I bite down and taste the blood spreading
between my teeth
She looks at me with odd horror.
As I pull hard against the metal jaws that once
were sinking into her
And are now sinking into me
I press my form into the cold steel and as I fill
the alien jaws with my flesh
She becomes free
I watch as she whimpers and limps back to the
wilds from which I came
The fox glances back over her shoulder as she
slips into the wilds
And I cannot follow
Now a prisoner of her past pain
I howl low and sweet
Strangely content that at least one walks free
Time passes
Moons rise and Moons fall
Tonight I hardly notice the pain
As my eyes linger on the wilds where she last
parted
and I am startled as I see the sly fox returning
slinking…
stalking towards me
This time my eyes hold the terror
I can hear the hunger within each of her soft
steps
She creeps across the distance

and I am helpless
Unable to run away
Just like she was
She leans in
Her breath warm and dangerous
She whispers
The wilds are still close
This time neither of us have to stay in the trap

Addictions

Spike me like the punch you drank last fall
When your hazy eyes looked away for the first
time
And have yet to discover the will to look back
Quick sound thunder
door slamming
The object of your affection just spilled away
Look
Here
Before the smoke
From our sharp wild flame
Disappears

Crumpled Paper

My head is spinning left
It's pulling here and there
All my thoughts are trite and maimed
So finish with some flair
Light the quick addiction
Finish off the chant
Fingers are now longing
the darkness from the plant
Caress the keys in silence
The faint and subtle noise
Gentle clicking symphony
The march of elder toys
Do not care for words
just letters in the bin
Wanting for the moment
Succulent the sin

Fear

Let me take you away
To my world of dreams
Spin you around like a thousand cinderellas
on a dance floor polished with tears
Ballroom pleasantries
With massive lean to fornicating Barbie dolls
all wearing their plastic wonder masks
pushing out their not-so-secret weapon lust
Showing just enough of their double-D mantraps
As we dance, you notice them
All staring at you
And why?
You are the wonderful everything different
just like they want to be
but can't
Because they are scared

Open Door

41

I no longer look up into the light
Like having no wind
And just the right kite
But reek it does
when it dies
Devoured by the child of flies
She who plays with elder toys
Misunderstanding the subtle ploys
Of souls that dance
And fall from grace
Calm raging heart and pretty face
Lonely friend
We are not accidental
You Swallowed me with your Darkness Gentle

Wind

42

I remember savoring a breeze
That bones can taste the ice in
It swept through
Penetrating endlessly
One million sharp needles
Leave a thousand hairs standing in place
And still I want
The effect of your breeze
Warm
Silent
Present
Built with unforgiving air
I want to walk through your life
And leave a chill

Sheets

Needing the air to clean the lungs
When the insight is my left eye tonight
And the bright embroidery of flowers fly
Can I stay enough to hold forever with you
I break and the poem flies
Slipping into the tracks of my memory
Evading the end where the steam engine roars
Through the wanting lover's night
Satin sheets stained with lust and passion
Cover the enthralling moonlit movements
Of two
And their dance to oblivion
when and where should I stand
at the end of their commotion

Audition

Hurry and break the cycle
Turn the stone
Till the putrid carving of a frown
Boils into something of a smirk
Belittling all the trite problems of place
Trying to find liberty
In this overdramatic movie life
Won't sink like some redone Titanic
Won't die like a Shakespearean love
Look to the stars
I am a supernova of thoughts
Believing in my own fairytale
Writing the plot till the stars turn to dust
And the ever afters happily come

Latte

Chocolate spills
Darkens to Mocha
Sugar runs
Removes bitterness
Drop vanilla
Spreads like butterfly memories
Milk Pours
Steam burns everything together
Your lips
taste the world but not the coffee

Muster

Pull away quick
And slide
This way or that
Spilling the atmosphere of bliss into some
drunken pond
Disgust the lilies with algae that sticks to your
precious toes
Perchance you can
And do
Get your feet wet
Would you decide the water is too rough to
swim
Or would you seem too cold in the month of
June
Look hard
One heart may bloom
Given the chance
Wait long
And enough
Time grants the courage

Americana

Watch the pendulum swing
Eight year movement
far left

far right

Sidled in American blight
We oppressed those who were us
Then broke ourselves on the yoke
Scrambled our morals with blood and oil
We called it freedom?
Freedom for the masters that have,
Slavery in chains of credit for those who don't
Blasphemer of patriotic dribble
We trade fear for lives
tear raw flesh till it hives
suckle the corroded teat of Lady Liberty
Till we are poisoned with copper and lead
keep draining her till she is but a husk of her
former self
Anorexic and malnourished
The masters are selling meat and poison
We have enough to buy
But not enough for the tax

Weeping Century

I see the sad eyes linger
As I board the train
Watered gaze
Broken by time's cruel fate
Discarded acidic yellow
Beaconing a taste
Bitter disappointment souring the stain
I wonder who you lost to find your silk dismay

Chasing the Dragon

I am the Dragon I was chasing
I have destroyed everything I have ever touched
I am cursed with life
Cursed with love
Cursed with touch
I feel and I don't
I see and I don't
I have sucked the world dry
inhaled all the beauty that has ever existed
smoked it into ash and soot and nothing
And all I own is pending pain
the seeds of life and change
the saplings of emptiness
The tree of wonder why I didn't stop
Tasting the fruits of my damage

There it Was

I watched for your love
but it never pulled into my driveway
I waited for your love
but it didn't get lost on the way
I wished for your love
but its star wasn't falling
I hoped for your love
and nothing happened
and there it was

In those three words

The three words I didn't tell you
The three words I was afraid to say
The three words I am saying now

I love you

Sugar in the Sauce

Since the first time I saw the sun dance in your
hair
I knew you were more than magic
But I never tried to taste you
Never let myself get close enough to your fire
Because even from a distance
You can still light up my eyes
Surely the fire of your soul could reduce me to
ashes
I am twisted in the knots of your ouroboros tail
This infinity of you that lingers in my voice
running around my mind
Breaking all my rules
Like the one about falling…
again
But I am still clinging to the moon
Too afraid to let go
Hoping you are falling
But I see you holding too
I am scared of winning
because I'm so damn good at losing
And all that cold fear
about falling from so high
breathes in the back in my chest

telling me to tighten the laces of my running
shoes and run away
Before I fall to earth
And shatter against the ground
I will not know how to fix me
because all my broken pieces
They will still feel like missing you
But every time I orbit you
I throw caution to the wind
Because every moment with you
Is worth the compound interest of that future
pain
Because I Love You
If you ever ask me
The moment that I knew?
It was the day we had dinner in a pasta shop
And you put sugar in the sauce
Anyone else…
I would have thought it strange
But there in that sun-drenched booth
It felt like it had always been this way
I suddenly knew
I loved watching you add sweetness to your
plate
Because it is something you do that makes you
happy
And there is nothing more breathtakingly
beautiful
In the past

In the present
In the universe

53

Than you happy

Tattoo

You are the ink on my skin
You are the stain on my heart
that I don't want to wash away
You are the breath in my sin
You bend light with your smile
Let me borrow your soul with my laugh
Since you stole mine with your eyes
If you give me your love
I'll give you mine
I'll take your picture by the lake
If the ocean is out of our reach
And we can pretend that we are happy
Until we are

Needed

The light that is needed
Burns within the darkest woods
It ignites the vines that ensnare the soul
Melting away the thorns that hold us back

The light that is needed
Illuminates the void
In the spaces between hope
Drawing in the faint flicker
Of weary travelers lost in the dark

The light that is needed...
Is You

Speak

Each time I speak
I hurt a little less
no
that isn't exactly right
The hurt does not change
But the pain screaming in my mind loses a little
volume
The ache stabbing at the broken pieces of my
heart loses a pulse
The hollow taking up all the space you used to
occupy echoes softer
the hurt does not change
I change

The Rental

I feel like I am in a rental, and they gave me a
model I did not reserve,
I got one with sharp bold features and ground
clearance and far too much horsepower,
I am pretty sure I ordered one with gentle
curves, that hugs the winding road, and purrs
when she is turned on,
They must have been out of what I reserved
when I picked up this model.
But they don't do exchanges and I've already run
up the mileage.
At some point, I must have taken the keys,
At some point, I must have said since you don't
have what I want…
Give me the easy option,
At some point, I must have said I'll take this one
because the sports package is too hard to learn,
It required learning how to shift far too early,
It required knowing when to keep the top up,
It required knowing when to evade "far too
much horsepower" when "far too much
horsepower" is out of control,
It required monthly maintenance,
The world would have expected daily detailing,
And let's face it, that is a lot of work,

And I am lazy,
This model is an automatic with a couple of
bells and a few whistles,
It will even drive itself if I let it, and I have.
It looked a lot better before the holes in the road
dented the fenders and muddied up the exterior,
It looked a lot better before I went off-road,
But the experiences I had off in the uncharted
wilderness have shown me that my engine will
purr if I let it,
And I have learned I can hug the winding road if
I just slow down,
I still don't have those gentle curves but I can
now celebrate you if you do,
If I wasn't me I would have learned how to
operate this model years ago,
But before now, I couldn't see over the dash and
press the gas pedal at the same time,
there wasn't enough of me to fill the driver's
seat,
Before now I wasn't comfortable with how easy
it is to crash into the other drivers on this road,
I did not know how easy it is to wreck this
machine,
Getting tangled in cars I shouldn't have danced
with,
Crashing into curves I wasn't ready for
and in doing so, breaking parts of the engine I
didn't know how to replace,

I wasn't drafting the cars I should have been
racing behind,
I wasn't riding with the cars I was comfortable
around,
I will admit a long time ago I tried to return it,
I was out of gas and I let the battery run down,
I decided to drain the fluids and abandon this
machine for a junkyard promised by a dealer I
didn't believe in,
Someone stopped by before I did and gave me
enough gas to make it to the next filling station
and a jump that kept me going long enough to
charge myself on my own,
The road since then has been
Beautiful but Broken,
Perfect but Painful,
I am thankful I didn't return this machine early,
I am now sure the whole reason I took the rental
is to get where I want to go in a model that isn't
mine.

Monsters

They lumber across nightmares,
Hulking forms with sharp teeth,
incisors built to tear flesh from bones,
Gnashing molars for crunching the less tender
bits.
Since their claws and teeth are not defensively
reinforced by thick hide and thicker fur,
They are offensive by nature,
And for all their ferocity and strength, the
monsters' deadliest weapon is their intelligence,
They design instruments for death,
They create poisons for creatures they believe
might harm them,
They create fire to burn bright and to burn
devastating,
And completely unnecessary, the monsters
design tools for torture,
These methods are used against all life, even
they themselves are not immune,
They are addicted to inflicting pain and Sorrow
on others and themselves,
Fear drives them to violence,
Eight-legged life is smashed with terror,
Six-legged life is crushed underfoot even when
the creature is benign.

Four-legged life is herded for mass graves of
hand-carved delicate chunks of once was alive
and beautiful,
while the less pretty bits are ground into wet
lumps to be packaged and shaped and held in
buildings till the monsters trade paper and
plastic so they can feed,
Two-legged life…. well the monsters have rules
for two-legged life,
There are rules when it is thousands against
thousands, all the way down to one versus one,
And the rules are not fair, and too often not
followed,
They roam the earth destructive and unchecked
by anyone but themselves,
They lash out at anything they don't understand,
And they don't understand a lot,
But these hulking terrors are not inherently evil.
They are merely human.
And these 'humans' have this one redeeming
capability, one hope—love.
Within love there is the possibility of kindness
and compassion and understanding,
A reason not to destroy but to create,
To create art, to create life, and to create words.
Words that teach these foul creatures to heal, and
to nurture, to grow and understand.
It is a subtle dance each time they meet another
creature,

An inner battle of fear versus love,
And they can love, if they can get past the fear,
It is against themselves that lies the greatest
challenge,
For it is terrifying to fall in love with a human,
Because we know, somewhere deep in our inner
being, we are in love with a monster.

Words are Sharp

We often wear armor because
Words are sharp
Some words puncture and leave scars you will
carry forever
And the deepest wounds are often left by the
ones who know the gaps in your shell
Words are sharp
Some words cut so deep your entire universe
falls through the slit and you can't understand
the weight of the nothing left behind
Words are sharp
Some words are so sharp they can cut entire
highways of intrusive thoughts out of your head
Leaving the darkness bleeding away
Words are sharp
Some words can cut the lens you view the world
from
Show you a different facet of life's gemstone
A perspective maybe you couldn't see before
because of the angle
A perspective maybe you couldn't see before
because the impurity of what was cut away
Words are sharp
I don't wear armor anymore
because I am ready for surgery

Attempted Flirtation

64

I was up late last night because of the moon
Her moonbeams pooling in the darkness
Her full body naked in the sky
Her orbit with earth
so erratic
it wobbles
like my knees when you walk by me

Center

Let me taste the center of your sin
arched back and curled toes
Exhaling the intimate noises that dwell inside
your secret garden
Let me trace your curves and edges like a river
traces the valley it belongs inside
Let me climb your peaks with my lips to a
height not attainable on earth
But found in the nirvana of your thirsty fingers
You are the heaven I swim in
Satin sheets twisted in shaking tremors
As I devour your invisible scars
Let me watch the cool silver moonbeams caress
your form
And I will follow her gentle instructions
Let me curl around your quaking body as the
pressure of the opposing forces of vulnerability
and desire erupt
Let me revel in your release
The earthquakes of you leveling the cities of
who I was before you.
Let me embrace you as the aftershocks fade and
settle
Let the night steal your grey eyes from me as
they drift softly into your dreams

And I will hold you
Till the stars fade
And the moon sinks
And the sunlight steals you away from me again

Read the Room

Read the room.
Look into the souls mingling in the space you
now share
Listen to the way they speak
their truths… bare, bold, and naked,
their lies, the ones hiding in shadows which
cover parts of themselves they are not yet ready
to reveal.
Read the room.
To see if you can speak the hard truths or if you
have to temper your words in the honey of their
gospel. Careful not to let them taste the
bitterness of ideas that might be truths,
Ideas that might cut into an armor made of gods
and virtues that fused with flesh and mind long
ago.
Your sharp words must cut carefully to open the
armor and not wound the beautiful soul within.
Read the room,
See if their magnificent eyes linger on the words
loss, longing, or *gone.*
If their eyes light up when the word *lover* passes
your lips or if those sad eyes start to water as
they savor the silk dismay,

that echo of emptiness stained with salt regret
and sweet memory,
Read the room,
because when you enter a room you change it.
You add yourself to an equation we will never
fully understand.
Because the math of adding coffee shops to
shades of blue and dividing it by the loneliness
you had last fall does not have an answer. It only
has a feeling.
Once you know that feeling…

Read for the room.

My Voice

It took me 45 years not to hate the sound of my
own voice.
I don't age quickly, and by that I mean
I age slowly
It is a gift. I see it now, but when you still don't
reach anyone's kneecaps and your voice is shrill
and tiny, it is hard to understand that peculiar
genetic trait as a gift.
It was at this miniature age I misunderstood the
world when my voice was criticized in a way my
tiny underdeveloped mind could not
comprehend as anything other than hate.
I loved to sing back then. My grandfather had
brought home a Japanese pop music tape
This tape was confiscated.
This was again misunderstood by my mind that
not only was my voice unpleasant but that I also
could not sing.
So I began to mimic the voices from the silver
screen—the cartoon characters that made people
smile, because I loved it when I could make
someone smile.
I would imitate anything that I saw as adored if I
could change my voice to match, because when I
was not me, I felt loved

But I got older, and around the time I learned to drive, my voice started to deepen and I could no longer mimic the voices I had invested so much time in.

I no longer could perform like before because I was changing, and I watched my feeble attempts draw disappointment across the faces of family and friends.

It reinforced my belief that my voice was noise to be tolerated.

Then when I was finally free of the nest and attempting to rebel and grow, I got my tongue pierced

The following three days my tongue became thick and swollen causing my words to fight through my teeth.

At a coffee house, a young man asked me with my swollen tongue to do a Scottish accent. The imitation Game was back on.

I began to imitate the voices of celebrities who were kind of famous, but time is a cruel mistress and my younger friends stopped recognizing the voices.

Some of the celebrities even became politicians, and the opportunities to showcase the stolen voices kept dwindling.

The world had been Ursula and I, the little mermaid, had willingly signed the contract to

give up my voice. The world would be better if I
was just quiet.

I was invited to Karaoke on a Thursday in the
spring of 24. I showed up to support a friend,
and I swore up and down I would not be singing.
I was sitting at a table near the stage filled with
liquid courage. A young woman got up to sing
"Pretty Woman" and as the song went on I found
myself belting out all the lyrics, and there on
that stage, this perfect human had lost the
rhythm of the lyrics. She asked me, in wild
pantomime, to get up on the stage and sing with
her, and I did. In that moment, she found my
missing voice, and she did the most amazing
thing with it. She gave it back to me. I began to
sing again.

I began to write again,

I began to speak again, and now wherever there
is an opportunity, because of her, I can give my
voice to you.

Your Art

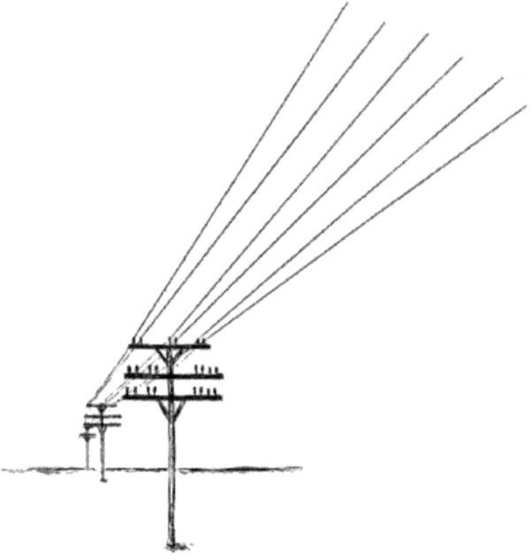

I love this space, and I love coming here,
The vibration of strings coming to life,
Your soft vocals of summer warming my soul.
I come for your music and I stay till the last set,
forgive the moments I give into my addiction
and sneak off for a cigarette,
I make sure to stay close enough to hear your art
wafting from inside the building.
You make music that my weary form needs to
hear.
Arrangements of artistic skill I can feel your
soul submerged within,
and I swim in the newness of your creation.
The life you paint spills out onto a canvas I
could spend eternity in, Young and Old alike

coming together to share heartbreak and hope,
humor and happiness.
Raw incredible talent honing itself on the
whetstone of performance.
You heal me with your art.
Let me elaborate so that the last line is felt as
strongly as my heart speaks it.
In the perfect spring my best friend willingly
stopped breathing the air that burned her soul.
So she doesn't live in the physical world
anymore.
She lives in my memories and the beats of my
heart.
She lives in my words.
She was my music, my ride-or-die. And we
would ride just to get her away from her
demons.
We would sing and laugh as the road and time
passed underneath us.
I see her on every long country road, the slender
white lines that reach out for a horizon she will
never see.
I see her in stop signs and curb checks.
I hear her in the pages of her favorite books.
I feel her in piano keys and soft vocal notes.
I taste her in every song that we sang together…
Her playlist was extremely long,
But with every new experience I heal,

With each new song the echo of her emptiness
grows softer,
And you bring such sweet songs with you,
You bring so much beautiful music,
All I bring are words, but you accept them.
So I will speak of the Moon and Monsters and
Men,
I will speak of your eyes and your voice and
your breath,
I will speak of the chords of your heart, the ones
you pluck each time you caress your guitar.
I will speak to you of the mysteries of the
universe, and time, and love.
My subtle way of imploring and begging for you
to create more of your art.
the art that kindles the fires in my soul,
And now, I will speak that last line again
You heal me with your Art.

She is Back in Time

She is the '90s preserved in a small frame
Swimming in the nostalgia of her once
happiness
Bic Runga, Debbie Gibson, and songs like "One
More Try"
We always do one more try
Hoping she won't come and go like she does
But she does
She slides into the familiarity of her sadness
Romancing the neglect she loves
And running to the soul bruises of "he doesn't
really love you"
I can't compete, unable to abuse her boundaries
Hoping one day I can light the fires in her eyes
again
Pull her passion back from the abyss it was
discarded into by Monsters who can't
comprehend the wonder she is
I observe as she attaches melancholy moments
to a time gone by
When she was happier and before she tangled
herself in my sorrow.
She is the '90s preserved in immaculate
perfection
So I watch with sweet sadness as she drifts away
Again

The Dive

We were standing in a parking lot when she said
she wanted to go skydiving,
I was reluctant, having a distant memory of
jumping from just a juvenile height once before,
and that left me bruised and stepping lightly for
weeks,
I have never fallen from this high before,
So, naturally, I leapt with wild abandon,
The first seconds hit me with so much vertigo
my stomach screamed amusement park rides,
And I was exhilarated by the suddenness of
acceleration, and I leaned all the way into the
fall,
Angling myself for the fastest descent,
Near weightlessness as I
plummeted back to the world that I had so
foolishly left,
Time stretched,
Had I been falling for 28 seconds or 28 years,
The reality of my world so immeasurably far
away filled me with dread
And I found myself paralyzed, unable to react to
what was happening,
And still I fell,
and I fell,

I, so afraid of falling, had not noticed the
distance I had raced, and a cold sweat took over
me,
Now long past the point I could have opened a
parachute,
Anxious that an impact from such a height
would crush me entirely,
Scattering my bones across the Earth,
I closed my eyes not wanting to see the end of
my existence,
Howling in my ears as I felt the end
rushing to greet me,
My skin stinging with anticipation,
My doomed soul fell,
my thoughts raced,
this can't be real,
I don't deserve this,
This can't be lo…

I love you.

the words leaving her tongue stopped time and
space,
My feet now barely touched the crust of the
earth, I was weightless in her words,
I opened my eyes and saw the universe dancing
inside hers,
There in that moment inches from her lips,
I had fallen farther than ever before,

I was not broken,
Not destroyed,
And more alive than I have ever been.

I can't Stop

I can't stop trains, so much mass, already in
motion,
Once the train gains so much speed I can't stop
it.
I can't stop bullets, little flecks of death,
Once fired, the damage is irreversible. I can't
stop it.
I can't stop panic, so much fear,
Once the fear is rooted in the mind, I can't stop
it.
I can't stop hate, so much pain,
Once it claws its way into the world, it only
seems to escalate,
I can't stop it
I can't stop suicide
I cannot control the darkness in one's heart. I
cannot mend another's pain.
I can't stop it
But I can speak and warn that the train is coming
I can be a voice against violence
My words can calm the worry in your heart
I can say, "I love you"
If my words might heal one stitch of your soul
I can't stop

The First Word of the Poem

You

The Last Word of the Poem

81

Me

Kitchen

I cleaned the kitchen today.
There was a vase that held flowers from your
funeral, next to the glasses I drink water from
every day. I moved it to the highest shelf so I
can only see it when I am looking up.
Moved some dirty socks from the table that
didn't match. I am not even sure how they got
there.
I started boiling some water for tea.
I looked for a mug and found an old one with a
bear printed over the words "Merry Christmas."
I thought of you and how much you loved
Christmas. It had a hairline crack in the bottom
of it. So I gingerly placed it in the trash.
The silverware drawer was a mess,
So I took out all the utensils I feed myself with
and placed them back in the drawer in some
semblance of order.
The Kettle whistle blew and I poured the boiling
water into a pitcher. I added the tea.
I found some lids that don't have matching jars
anymore. I paused because they reminded me
that I was also an incomplete set. I threw them
away too.
I took out the tea infuser and let the tea rest.

I took the clothes from the last camping trip I
was on and moved them from a dining chair to
the laundry hamper.
I took another mug from the cabinet
Poured myself a cup of tea
Sat down in the kitchen chair.
And looked up, I saw the beautiful etching on
the vase from your funeral.
And today I didn't fall apart

Coastline

I haven't figured out love
I fall in love all the time
constantly falling
constantly breaking
I have broken my heart so many times
There are no shards of glass left to cut you
My heart is sand
And sand is irritating
It gets into places you didn't think sand could get
into
You need an ocean to rinse off all that irritating
sand
And love is an ocean
My sand is constantly beaten by the crashing
waves of the ocean
I am the beach
Do you still love the beach?

Weight of Words

There is power in words, a sort of magic that
separates us from mere beasts.
Words are the shape of thoughts spilled into the
universe to echo the heart.
Words can bind a person to a belief, or set them
free from one.
Words can imprison a person from being
themselves or free them to be their true self
Words can shatter a soul, or mend a heart.
Words can change a generation,
Words can topple governments,
Words can kill Gods…
I see a few faces of doubt about that last one.
Over two thousand years ago a man killed an
entire pantheon of gods with the word Love.

Heartcastles

Who am I
I am a kid playing beside the ocean making
sandcastles
Is that who I am
Or who I was
Is that one of my happiest memories
Or just a moment in time before the 27 years
that she existed
Back when I knew the answers. Because the
questions were easy.
My favorite dinosaur?
The Tyrannosaurus Rex
What do you collect,
I collect stones and stories.
What am I afraid of?
Back then it was probably dogs, or horses
Now it is waking up in a world without her in it
I wake up to my fear every morning
I loved watching her light when she talked about
what she loved
She was passionate about everything she loved
My favorite thing in the entire universe was
watching the stardust in her eyes ignite
And her eyes held the most spectacular fire
Now that her fire is no longer here…

I am cold
I am shattered
My heart broke so completely the pieces no
longer have edges
My heart is sand
Miles of sand
So, Who am I?
Now that she is gone…
I am a person with a little Sad
like a cute little puppy
When I say puppy I mean small one like a fully
grown Great Dane who is half the size of a horse
When I say half the size of a horse
I mean twice the size of a house
And when I say puppy
I mean a Tyrannosaurus Rex
A Tyrannosaurus Rex with all his sharp hungry
teeth ready to devour what is left of my soul
When I say Tyrannosaurus Rex
I mean the Ocean
The Ocean of love that used to crash on my
shore
I dove into it and forgot how to swim and now
its dark depths are grief
And by the ocean I mean the night sky
The vast dark void
And by the night sky
I mean the entire universe
This great empty universe

I have a small Sad the size of the entire universe
But you are stars…. moments of light against
my echo of emptiness
You are out there lighting the darkness for those
who are lost
Who am I
I am lost
Playing beside an ocean of grief
A little Sad sitting faithfully beside me
Trying to make castles with the sand of my heart

To the Capricorn

Sorry
I don't date Capricorns
It is not that I won't appreciate your intensity
Or your passion
It is not that I can't adore your refreshing
honesty
It is not that I won't cherish your effortless
sensitivity
The inviting way you will accept me as I am
Already, I am wary of your perfect persistence
Your beautiful determination
In fact I will fall for everything you are
I will not be able to resist admiring your resolve
I will delight in supporting your ambitious
dreams
I will probably love you instantly
It is not that I don't want to date you
It's just every time you do the things that I love
so very very much about you
Her form will pass behind my eyes
Every time you argue your point
So perfectly articulated that I will have to
concede
Her triumphant smile will play in my memories
I know how incredibly amazing you are

So I choose not to chain down your heart with
mine
Because, all those wonderful moments where
you are your best you
I won't be able to completely pay attention to
your light
Part of me will always admire her phantom
The shadow of her absence created by your
dancing radiance
and I will not be able to Love you completely
Which is the only way to love you
I am sorry
My best friend still reigns over your
constellation
and I…
I am still in love with her ghost

Starshine

Who are you, as lump of wet carbon
to be ruled by stars
Those vague points of light against the void
Do those majestic burning suns
know the inner workings of your heart and soul
Can you, as so much forgotten stardust
Claim to hear the voices of distant stars?
Can you, as a minute grain of life
Believe that the stars that witnessed your birth
are actively guiding you?
Can you, a cosmic entity
Pretend to be connected by time and purpose to
such distant power and radiance?
You can…
And that choice is the greatness of existence
The beauty of life
This perfect unknowing of what is the truth
behind our turmoil
The choice
To seek truth and light
And revel in deceit and darkness
It is the fine line you dance across as a subtle
flicker of a long-dead star
You are her final breath

A memento of eons past when a magnificent star
sacrificed herself in a fiery display of power
And you were born from her ashes
You are not merely stardust
You are life
Proof that the star existed
And that she died
It is the reason you crave to devour all the
textures and colors
That create this experience known as living
You are the melody which echoes the story of
her
Because you are the fabric of the universe
You are starshine

Horn Blower

If I told you I was the end of the world
When my song plays
The stars fall from the night sky
Sinking the suns
Blotting out the night Sky with darkness
Would you lose hope?
Let that hope wither and die on a Vine
Grapes that died and turned into raisins in the
the suns
The suns that died in the night
While you were looking for answers
You watch the moon fall into the Sea
Swallowed up by darkness
Hiding in the deep crushing sorrow
When she embraced me as the moon sank
And the silver coin of her perfect form dances
Just out of breath hidden by waves of tears
With the marionettes who dance with strings
Pulled by the puppets
Who are controlled by Angels
Who were dancing with the Gods?
Gods who are falling over themselves
Trying to find a way to keep a grip on the world
That was not made for men
That was not made for women.

Was made for time.
Was Made for the end,
When the suns fell and we were swallowed by
the darkness.

Vintage

Drink with me
One more time
Tell me that I am love
And you are wine
And I will whine that your love is too strong and
sweet
but the fingers form so nicely around the edge of
the glass
This cup of you that is so fragile and holds the
song of your creation
I lean in close and breathe you in
floral notes of you
And the hint of charcoal from the burning
cinders of my heart
I look into the depths of you
And there in the mirror surface
Spilling into my eyes is you
Universes of your dreams dance into me
Escaping the prison you held them in
I am not looking for bed Chambers or satin
sheets
I am not looking for skin, or bones, or perfection
I am looking…
For you.
Skin will age and wrinkle

And time will damage everything you are made
of
Pieces of you will become less perfect
According to standards written by men who do
not understand
Every day that goes by…
You become richer, bolder, more complex
and so, the bottle so dusty
Sun weary and vintage has greater worth
To witness you as you become more than the
vines and the land had to offer
I long to taste a glass of your time

Edge of time

And it is in this quandary of life,
this mystery of breaking the end of time.
I was at the edge of time
I was positive that you would be here.
Long after I died.
Scorpions of your stars in my veins, stinging
every inch of everything I have ever been.
I am so sure that in this alien world, I am a
stranger like you were.
And I walk in the darkness that blankets these
somber lands,
Because of you, it does not rain within the
hallowed Halls of my heart.
My heart, that now descends willingly into the
shadowed woods,
to walk as a light, a beacon, a blaze,
A fire that still singes the Shadows that shroud
your kind eyes.
Pulling at your perfect soul, wrapped in so much
sadness, so much Darkness, so much self-doubt,
self-loathing, and so much fear.
Is that what we become? If we are without love.
We cannot heal if we cannot love ourselves.
And who will teach us to love ourselves
If we cannot see love around us.

How can we learn if pain is our teacher,
Borrow my eyes, and look at the person I see.
I will not call you perfect, but your curves and
edges paint warmth in my core,
Every time I see you, every time I smile, every
time my voice leaves my body,
Every word says I love you.
Every action speaks I accept you.
With every beat of my heart,
I give you love.

Poetry is a Beast

Poetry is a Beast
She has been chewing the soft tissue of my heart
and clawing her way through my rib cage
Poetry is a Beast
I have wrestled with her for decades trying to
keep her blind and quiet
Poetry is a Beast and I am losing the battle of
telling her that she was not worth the air she
needed to breathe.
Poetry is a Beast
that wants to be free, free of my ribs, free of my
heart
Poetry is a Beast
Who stalked the dark forests of my soul
A darkness that only existed because I kept her
inside
behind closed doors and shuttered windows.
Poetry is a Beast
That devours my invisible scars, and she
hungers for yours
Poetry is a Beast
who demands justice when she is witness to
inequity,
colorblind she can only see the colors of your
soul,

Poetry is a Beast
When she is prowling your mind she does not
rest,
and she has been quiet for far too long.
She is ready to howl.
Poetry is a Beast
she is made from the raging fire in your heart
and those flames consume my soul
Poetry is a Beast
She stares into the river of my eyes
the raging rapids of my soul
Poetry is a Beast
she is love
Poetry is a Beast
she is pain…
Poetry is a Beast
And She is me.

One Day

It was us against the world,
Or… it was us against her depression,
Or… it was us against time,
Time and One Day
One day we were going to go out west and be
actors,
One day we were going to produce a musical,
One day we were going to write a play,
One day we were going to go to a concert,
One day we were going to read books in a park,
One day…
There were a lot of one days for us,
I wasn't ready for the one day when flowers, a
plaque, and a gentle mound of dirt in a cemetery
would become my best friend.
Some days I forget that she is gone,
I get lost in a fog.
There is this blur where I distract myself,
And in that blur I almost miss the people who
shine light into the world,
Like you,
And I almost didn't see you,
Which is odd because you radiate more light
than is available in the room,
That should be impossible.

And how did I forget the taste of your name?
Because your name feels like sunlight and
sounds like the ocean.
The ocean of words hiding behind the iceberg
blue of your eyes.
And when I asked when I would hear your
words,
you replied "One day."
Before you spoke those words, for me one day
was buried,
You helped me realize that I didn't bury one day
with her,
All of those one days still exist,
just different, just mine.
You gave me back one day,
and tomorrow,
and every day,
With what you did with just two words,
I soak in the anticipation of what the rest of your
words will do…

One day.

She Moves

She is there in the back of the crowd,
And she moves,
The music bends the air, the crowd listens,
And she moves,
The guitars pluck vibration in the air.
And she moves,
Her silhouette against the city is righteous,
And she moves,
Her smile is radiant, her soul is soft,
And she moves,
She is soooo beautiful when she moves.

Sad Poetry

I don't write sad poems when I'm with you,
You turn sunsets into sunrises and nights into
stars and moonbeams
The songs are sweeter when you sing them.
I want to kiss you the way the cool breeze off
the lake kisses your skin.
And I forget to take pictures because how can I
capture a dream?
This dream, so vivid and complex, can't fit in a
frame

The Bridge Unburned

There is a bridge,
Moss-covered and forgotten
The way to its edge is hidden
The earth whispers directions
with foxes trails and deer paths
The cautious path is guarded
poisonous plants and unstable hungry earth
The bridge stands decaying
A river uncrossable below
Gentle currents of Memories
And rapids of forgetfulness
I step softly on the rotten beams
run my fingers over the indentation
She carved with her selfish hands
Her initials mark the middle
The point where I dare not pass
She has crossed over
And I cannot set fire to the only bridge I have
left of her love
But this bridge is unstable
Her bridge is unsafe
I wander back to the quiet places
Following the trails left by animals wiser than I
I watch the sun fall behind the forgotten bridge
For it is not my time to cross the bridge
unburned

The Apprentice

I took to tutelage from a master of love,
I learned more about love from her in 200 days,
Than I learned from
every book I ever devoured,
every play I ever enjoyed,
every movie I ever watched,
every song I ever listened to,
in my first 16,739 days.
One day love may find me again,
For now I am practicing the love that was found
in her lessons,
Love of seeing and accepting,
For that is love.
There lies no expectations, no attachments, no
need, no desire,
It is just love.
To see you
To accept you as you are presented
In this she was a master.
She would see your flaws and virtues and just
love them,
Perhaps it was her resignation from life that
allowed such a clear and unobstructed view.
She never judged anyone but herself,
And she was her harshest critic,

I am taking the last lesson she left,
The lesson I was forced to discover without her,
To see and accept the self,
My self,
I am borrowing your eyes and her eyes,
because mine are distorted with expectations,
Her eyes accept me as I am in this moment,
Your eyes allow love to flow like light,
And I am changed as I am observed,
Free of the attachments that bind love up on the
way to the soul.
My universe is now borderless,
Because you are an entire universe,
and here in this space, this multiverse, there is
infinite love.
And love persists despite the violence of her
end.
Even now I mourn the loss of my master,
And I am burdened with her violent legacy,
As I forgive her final selfish act,
And become more love than I was as Her
apprentice.

Insanity

One definition of insanity is doing the same
thing over and over
again, and expecting a different result.

Love is insanity.
Therein lies the magic of love,
Because love is doing the same thing over and
over,
and you never get the same result.
There was always a Twist…
A difference.
Every time you smack rock with the stick,
the same thing will happen.
The Rock will move or the stick will break.
Each time you love a person, it will be different.
But it hurt this time, you say.
It will hurt every time.
There will always be a sting, or an ache.
Love has a way to dig and carve into your heart
and cut pieces of you out.
And love gets into you differently,
It is not always cupid's little arrow,
Sometimes it's a trebuchet,
A massive harpoon stops your heart,
and you are lifted off of the ground,

and you soar through the air.
Sometimes you hit a wall and become pinned
like a butterfly,
on the wall of her memories,
But for me the best love is not delivered by
projectiles,
Sometimes love happens slowly over time,
the love that sneaks up on you,
Because the vines that crawl from their lips,
fit so neatly in your veins,
You no longer know where you end,
and they begin.

She Moves the Air

She moves the air
her lungs dispel the awful spell of uncertainty
Her vibrating chords of magic cast hope and
love in the room
as a couple dances in the back
and a brass saxophone seduces
the neon-lit stucco
dotted with the exclamation of the snare drum
and the sweetness of a bass guitar
the symbol shakes and spills into the room
The many versions of me sit in awe as the world
stops
And in this moment purchased by time
breaks the loop
And creates the circle
This art crescendos the human expression
And the saxophone
Like life
Plays on

This City

The cool air dances across warm forgotten skin,
Signs begging for money flicker in neon and
streetlight glow,
Wobbling through the streets.
Paved earth that invites you to her parlor,
I fell in love with her before she fell in love with
me.
She is just the right amount of broken,
maybe a bit too violent,
but with the right amount of love and loneliness,
the bus cuts across 39th
and a girl with Wendy's hair steps on after me,
an awkward smile passes my lips, beautiful in its
timid loneliness,
the bus lurches across potholes and
imperfections,
and a man in a green backpack texts someone
who makes him smile,
I watch as he waits for the next line of words to
cross the screen.
those letters…
more important than his stop.
The red light causes a pause as the promise of
cheesecake disappears on the right.

Is there hope in the screens that everyone is
absorbed in
Myself engaged in literary thumb exercises
as a couple scurries a crosswalk
the bus leans to the right and the seat next to me
is dirty
an unidentified weird brown thing left behind by
an unknown person.
I waltz past home towards my usual Thursday
routine.
The place where my voice was found,
There, in neon and dim lighting, a symphony of
other voices awaits.
Where poetry hides behind notes and
instruments.
And I wander past French pretension on 55th
Street.
Quaint shops and the smell of tea
And the struggle of a selfie
I offer assistance and forget I am at least two
sheets to the wind.
I snap a few pictures and I can see the beauty of
their souls.
I realize the pretension is mine, and not theirs.
The clarity of blurry vision and a self that has
learned to grow
From the love of a city,
That I am only now realizing..
This City, She loved me first.

Flames

There is a burning in the lungs
A crackling in the heart
The flames raging in dark pages
The cinders playing their part
Four hundred and fifty-one degrees of
everything I ever spoke
disappearing from my sharpened tongue
in ash and sparks and smoke
I can't stop or drop since I am now the fire
roll up another flaw
Put it on the pyre
Now that I am the light
Swimming in the drought
Now that I am fire
Nothing can put me out

My Plate

My plate is filled with nothing today
You can try it
But you need to use your imagination
It is not a void
It is not an absence
My nothing tastes like the finest teas
Served with Raggedy Ann and Andy and the
Earl of Grey
My nothing is served in pink plastic tea cups
My nothing tastes like limitlessness
My nothing tastes like strawberry dreams on
small plates
My nothing is everything if you believe
And you can try everything...
at least once

The Guest

I like movies,
I loooove movies,
like I am the person who waves back at the actor
on the silver screen
One of my favorite movies is *Extremely Loud &*
Incredibly Close,
I never felt a movie so strong
Like I am not autistic
Like my uncle wasn't autistic
like my sister is
See I was just labeled dumb until they labeled
me smart
and then gave up on me
I found the world doesn't care if a snare drum
hurts
So I found cigarettes
Self-diagnosis:
nails in a coffin to treat the imminent funeral
Self-medication
Side effects include
short-term humanity
lightheadedness
nausea (only the first time)
yellow teeth
bad breath

the need to escape to decompress in my own
smoke
Besides I've always loved playing with fire
Fire moves and lives like I want to,
It doesn't care what anyone thinks it can
consume anyone
It can multiply

The snare drum still hurts
It is extremely loud and incredibly close
I am not autistic because you have to pay for
that understanding
I am just easily overwhelmed
And overly sensitive to a few wavelengths
The saxophone can help
As long as it isn't a high G
The bass guitar helps the soothing vibration
but the sound is fast and loose, shaking my
nerves
I should have brought earplugs
I knew I would need them
But there wasn't enough room in my pockets
And I am vain
I also need room for the smoke
The heady acrid sharp flavors
They remind me that life is worth living
And that death
Death is still coming
And she can moan as I keep going

She can watch
And kiss me after I am done

Ghost Pains

When we lose a part of ourselves there is this
odd occasional pain

A ghost pain

A reminder that there is a part of us that we are
missing
I never thought I would know what that was like

Until I felt my heartbeat

And I realized

I amputated my own heart
when she amputated her life
Was that flutter her ghost holding me..

Or was that life

Three Two One   Clear

was that life

Three Two One   Clear

was that love

Thump
                thump
thump
                    thump

was that you

Again

Three Two One ….

                        Clear

was that me

Coming back to life

Coming back to love